Fact Finders®

Teachers, that means Laugh Out Loud.
Yup, science can be hilarious!

LOL Physical Science

The SOLID TRUTH about MATTER

by Mark Weakland
illustrated by Bernice Lum

Don't let his name fool you.
He's not weak. He's super
smart AND funny! And he's
probably pretty strong too.

A way important science guy who
made sure Mark didn't mess up.
His friends call him Al.

Consultant:
Alec Bodzin
Associate Professor of Science Education
Lehigh University
Bethlehem, Pennsylvania

CAPSTONE PRESS
a capstone imprint

Fact Finders are published by Capstone Press,
1710 Roe Crest Drive, North Mankato, Minnesota 56003.
www.capstonepub.com

Library of Congress Cataloging-in-Publication Data
Weakland, Mark.
The solid truth about matter / by Mark Weakland ; illustrated by Bernice Lum.
 p. cm.—(Fact finders. LOL physical science.)
Includes bibliographical references and index.
 Summary: "Describes what matter is and how it works through humor and core
science content"—Provided by publisher.
ISBN 978-1-4296-8427-9 (library binding) — ISBN 978-1-4296-9302-8 (paperback)
ISBN 978-1-62065-239-8 (ebook pdf)
1. Matter—Juvenile literature. I. Lum, Bernice, ill. II. Title.
QC173.36.W327 2013
530—dc23   2011051566

Editorial Credits
Jennifer Besel, editor; Tracy Davies McCabe, designer; Svetlana Zhurkin, media
     researcher; Laura Manthe, production specialist

Photo Credits
Dreamstime: Design56 (measuring cup), 22; iStockphoto: Gary Davison, 19 (top), Igor Djurovic,
18, Stacey Walker (frame), cover and throughout; Shutterstock: Albo003 (glass), 25, Alexey
Bragin, 6, ampFotoStudio (chocolate), 22, Anita Patterson Peppers (flour), 22, april70, 10 (bottom
back), Arsen (molecule background), cover and throughout, blue67design (flower), 25, Brux,
10 (top), chaika (fish), 20, 21, 32, charobnica, 9 (top), Danny E. Hooks (sugar), 22, Digital N
(math signs), 22, dmiskv, 27 (bottom), Dumitru Bogdan Enache (wood), 25, Elenamiv, 13 (back),
ensiferum (wave), 20, EuToch (oil), 22, graphit, 19 (bottom left), Gregory Gerber (eggs), 22,
gresei (ice cubes), cover, 11, 15, Hamik (map), 7, Irina Nartova (music note), 11, Jaimie Duplass,
17 (top right), Kim Reinick, 22 (right), mart (pencil scribbles), cover and throughout, Miguel
Angel Salinas, 15, Mikhail Dudarev (cows), 28, Mopic (billboard), 28, Odua Images (girl), 25,
OK-SANA (rain), 20, oksix, 8, Olga Tropinina (arrows and speech bubbles), cover and throughout,
R. Gino Santa Maria, 17 (top left), Skyline (notebook sheet), cover and throughout, Tetyana
Zhabska, 21, tuulijumala (explosion), 3 and throughout, ucla_pucla, 19 (bottom right), vector-RGB
(snow), 20; Svetlana Zhurkin, 16

Printed in the United States of America in Brainerd, Minnesota.

032012   006672BANGF12

TABLE (of) CONTENTS

Suuuuper Matter!

It is a speeding bullet. It is a powerful locomotive. It is the tall building leapt in a single bound.

It's matter!

Matter is a superhero that makes human life possible. But it exists far beyond human beings. Cars, stars, candy bars ... they're all made of matter. Everywhere you look, matter's there. Without matter, nothing would exist, not even you.

Matter comes in different forms. People are a wondrous combination of solid, liquid, and gaseous matter. Our well-toned muscles and rock-hard bones are solid matter. Liquid matter? About 5 pints (2.4 liters) of blood flow through a person's body. Special fluids surround and cushion our brains. And our flexible bladders hold almost 2 cups (0.5 L) of urine. As for gas, about 2 pints (0.9 L) of air exit your lungs with every breath. Gas exits other places too. But we won't talk about that.

gaseous—in the form of a gas

It's pretty clear that matter is everywhere. But what IS matter? Turn this matter-filled page to find out.

Chapter 1

Rockin' Matter

No, we couldn't think of a better title.

Matter is everywhere, but what exactly is it? Matter is stuff you can touch. To understand it better, let's list its basic properties.

For starters, matter takes up space. It's easy to see how your teacher takes up space. Air, which is invisible, also takes up space. To prove it, blow a few breaths of air into a balloon. The air you blow in takes up space. It causes the balloon to expand.

Insert your own teacher joke here. We're not getting in trouble for this one.

In addition, all matter has mass. Mass is the amount of stuff in an object. Because matter is made of stuff that takes up space, matter can be weighed and measured.

Hey, shadow! What's as big as an elephant but doesn't weigh anything?

Think about a rock. Does it take up space? Can you weigh it? Yes! How about a shadow? Nope. A shadow does not take up space, has no mass, and it cannot be weighed. So a shadow is not matter.

an elephant's shadow

Matterland

Matter on Earth is usually in one of three states. No, not Texas, Florida, or Alaska! We're talking about the form matter takes. Matter comes in solid, liquid, and gas states. Whether you're in Kentucky or Idaho, there's solid matter to walk upon and hold. There's liquid matter to swim in and drink. And there's gassy matter, such as air to breathe.

It's Atomic!

To understand the forms matter takes, we have to know what matter is made of. Matter's basic building blocks are small particles called atoms. Too tiny to see even with a microscope, atoms are bonded together. Atoms bond together because they are attracted to one another. When atoms bond to each other, a molecule is formed. All matter is made of molecules. When trillions of atoms collect in billions of molecules, they form matter you can see.

Our group of molecules is 4 billion strong. We've got to look huge by now!

Elementary Science

Sometimes molecules of all the same type bond together. When this happens, they create an element. For example, the element carbon contains only carbon atoms. The graphite in your pencil is made of carbon. Iron, silver, and gold are also elements.

If #2 pencils are so popular, why aren't they #1?

bond—the exchange or sharing of electrons by atoms to form a molecule
attract—to pull something toward something else

Periodic Table of Elements

Group - IUPAC
Group cas

Atomic number — 19
Symbol — K
Relativ atomic mass — 39.098
Potassium
Element name

Nonmetals
- Other nonmetals
- Halogens
- Noble gases

Metals
- Alkali metals
- Alkaline earth metal
- Lanthanoids
- Actinoids
- Transition metals

- Metalloids
- Post - transition metals

1	2											13	14	15	16	17	18
H																	He
Li	Be											B	C	N	O	F	Ne
Na	Mg											Al	Si	P	S	Cl	Ar
K	Ca	Sc	Ti	V	Cr	Mn	Fe	Co	Ni	Cu	Zn	Ga	Ge	As	Se	Br	Kr
Rb	Si	Y	Zr	Nb	Mo	Tc	Ru	Rh	Pd	Ag	Cd	In	Sn	Sb	Te	I	Xe
Sc	Ba	La - Lu	Hf	Ta	W	Re	Os	Ir	Pt	Au	Hg	Tl	Pb	Bi	Po	At	Rn
Fr	Ra	Ac - Lr	Rf	Db	Sg	Bh	Hs	Mt	Uun	Uuu	Uub	Uut	Uuq	Uup	Uuh	Uus	Uuo

La	Ce	Pr	Nd	Pm	Sm	Eu	Gd	Tb	Dy	Ho	Er	Tm	Yb	Lu
Ac	Th	Pa	U	Np	Pu	Am	Cm	Bk	Cf	Es	Fm	Md		

Periodically Tabled

Scientists made a chart of all the known elements called the periodic table. The chart shows every element's nickname. Scientists use these short names instead of writing out each element's long name.

Coming Together

A more complex kind of molecule is a compound. Sometimes different atoms bond with one another. These bonds form compounds. When two hydrogen atoms (H_2) bond with one oxygen atom (O), the compound water (H_2O) is created. When one carbon atom bonds with one oxygen atom, the result is carbon monoxide (CO). CO is an odorless, colorless, and dangerous gas. It's given off when gasoline is burned in engines.

It's surprising, but this is not the gas that comes out of your brother. That gas is a different kind of dangerous.

Just Bonded!

A Tight Bond

So what makes matter solid, liquid, or gas? The answer is in the bonds. Molecules of a solid are held together tightly by their bonds. Think of an ice cube. Within the cube, millions of water molecules are vibrating like bees in a crowded hive. The buzzing bees have no room to move. The water molecules in an ice cube are like those bees. Packed in and held tightly, water molecules in an ice cube can't easily move about.

All Wet

The bonds of liquid molecules are looser than in solids. Liquid molecules are like a cloud of bees flying about in a small room. The bees are still crowded, but there's room to flow around.

Molecules in a liquid move. This movement is why you can splash your hand into a bucket of water. Slide your hand into water, and the molecules move aside. If you did that with a block of ice, however, the **rigid** water molecules might just give you a bruise. ←

We do not recommend trying this at home.

Excuse you!

Hey, I'm vibrating here!

Jeez! Just 'cause we don't have a tight bond, doesn't mean you can just come between us.

Actually, it kind of does.

rigid—stiff and difficult to bend

Give Me Some Space

What about the bonds in gas molecules? Gas molecules move fast, just like bees flying outside. There's a lot of space in a gas because its molecules are far apart. Occasionally gas molecules collide, but they do not interact (or sting.)

We might have taken this bee thing a little too far.

Chapter 2

Solids and Liquids and Gases! Oh, My!

Atomic bonds determine what state matter is in. But we can't see those bonds. We can see matter's physical properties, though. Solids, liquids, and gases all behave differently. We can observe those behaviors to know what state matter's in.

Let's start with solids. Think about a rock. Rocks always have a shape of their own. And no matter how hard you press on a rock, you can't change its **volume**. Also, no two rocks can share the same space. These properties are key features of all rocks—and all solid matter.

I'm pressing as hard as I can, but I can't make this rock any louder!!

You DIDN'T really THINK we were talking about HOW LOUD a rock is, right? If you DID, you'd better check the definition.

volume—the amount of space taken up by an object

14

Squeezing Gases

Gases are totally different from solids. A gas expands to fill the container it's in. Let's use steam as an example. When a small amount of steam is released into a room, the gas molecules scatter everywhere. You'll find them in the corners, near the ceiling, and at the floor. Because gases expand, they physically take up a lot of space.

Gases are easy to compress too. This means a certain amount of gas can be squeezed into a small space. In contrast, liquids and solids are much more difficult to compress. Just try squeezing a large amount of milk into a small glass. Or try squeezing a bowling ball.

Now you know why "passing gas" can clear out a whole room.

Yeah, we know we haven't talked about liquid properties yet. Turn the page, and we'll get there.

Comparing States of Matter

solid   gas   liquid

15

Flowing Liquids

Liquids have special properties too. For example, a liquid's shape is always changing. A liquid takes on the shape of the container it's in. Liquids also flow. But they don't all flow at the same rate. Water poured from a jar flows quickly. Pancake syrup flows more slowly. Honey flows slowest of all.

How slowly or quickly a liquid flows depends on its viscosity. Viscosity is how much **friction** there is between a liquid's individual molecules. The more friction there is, the slower the flow.

Liquid is always changing to fit in. But you don't have to do that. Bee yourself! (OK, now we're totally done with the bee jokes.)

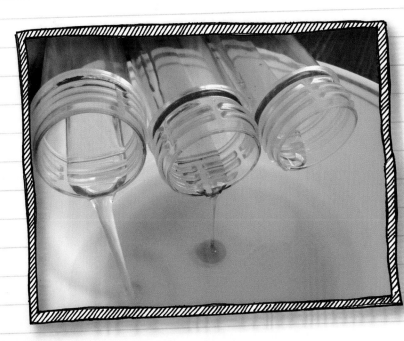

friction—a force created when two objects rub together; friction slows down objects

16

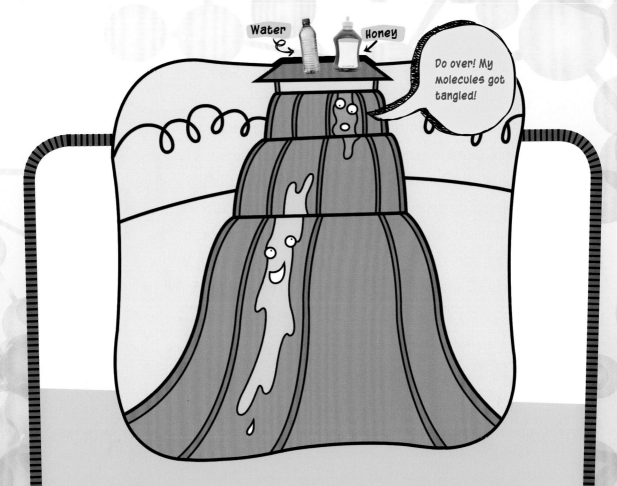

Why do some molecules have more friction than others? One reason is the shape of the molecules. Water, which flows quickly, is made from small, simple molecules. This means it's easy for water molecules to move and flow. Other liquids, such as honey, have large, complex molecules. When you pour this type of liquid, the molecules get tangled up. Molecules must untangle before the liquid can flow.

It's like untangling from the bed sheets before you can rush to the bathroom.

I'm Changing in Here!

Now that you know the properties of matter's states, let's confuse you. All matter can change from one state to another! Yes, that's right. All matter can be a solid, liquid, or gas. But changing states is way easier for some than it is for others. The bonds of carbon molecules are rigid and won't change easily. But the bonds of a water molecule enable it to easily change between states.

We have no idea how werewolves change. Don't ask.

Matter needs **energy** to change. This energy is usually in the form of heat. Place an ice cube in a pan. The warmth of the room will weaken the bonds between the water molecules. Soon the solid ice melts into a puddle of liquid. You see, when heat is added to a solid, the solid changes to a liquid. If it's hot enough, even rock or steel will become a flowing fluid.

Now add more energy to change states again. Put the pan of water on the stove, and crank the burner to high. The heat causes the bonds between the molecules to weaken even more. Rapidly moving water molecules begin to rise into the air. The liquid water changes to a gas called water vapor.

Don't do this without permission, or you will change the state of your mother's mood.

energy—the ability to do work, such as moving things or giving heat or light

Life Cycle of a Snowman

Snowmen thrive in cold, frosty areas of the world. But when they experience a gain or loss of heat, they must change in order to survive.

LIQUID (water)

freezing or solidification

melting or liquification

condensation

evaporation

sublimation

sublimation

SOLID (ice)

GAS or VAPOR (clouds/steam)

That's just a fancy word that means to go from a solid straight to a gas or vice versa. Do not pass through liquids. Do not collect $200.

Weather Water

Water is the most plentiful type of matter on Earth's surface. It's a unique type of matter because it easily exists as a solid, liquid, or gas. Think about the weather and the precipitation that comes with it. Snow, hail, sleet, and ice are examples of water in a solid state. Rain and drizzle? They're water in a liquid state. Fog and clouds are water vapor, which is nothing more than water in a gas state.

That's why we keep talking about water. It's not just because we're too lazy to think of another example.

They always say to dress for the water.

That's not what they say.

Water moves from state to state in a cycle. What kind of a cycle? Not a motorcycle! ← It moves in a water cycle. Here's how it works. Liquid water on Earth evaporates into the atmosphere as a gas. Water vapor forms clouds. The vapor then condenses into liquid water and falls to Earth as rain. If the air is cold, the precipitation takes the form of a solid such as snow. If the snow falls on warm ground, it returns to its liquid state. Liquid water gathers in rivers, lakes, and oceans. Then the cycle starts all over again.

Is that gas coming from you?

You really think my farts can change the state of matter?

Chapter 3

Mixin' in the Kitchen

Look around your kitchen. There you'll see sweet liquids freezing into solid Popsicles, solid ice cream melting into a liquid mess, and liquid water boiling into gaseous steam.

Matter is often in a state of change. One type of change occurs when matter is mixed. Take brownie batter for example. Start with some solids—chocolate bars, flour, and sugar. Next add the liquids—eggs, some water, and a bit of oil. Mix it up and, presto, it's brownie batter. It's also mixed matter. Bake this thick chocolaty gloop in the oven and what happens? It solidifies into a slab of mouth-watering brownies.

solids

liquids

Mmm, matter

Heat

What did the peanut butter say to the jelly?

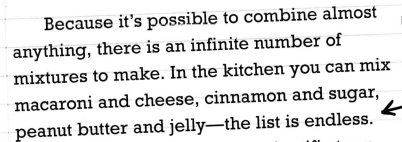

Mix with me, and we'll go places!

Because it's possible to combine almost anything, there is an infinite number of mixtures to make. In the kitchen you can mix macaroni and cheese, cinnamon and sugar, peanut butter and jelly—the list is endless.

Peanut butter mixes with everything! Mayo, chocolate, bananas, potato chips ...

The word "mixture" is a scientific term. Cinnamon and sugar or cereal and milk are called physical mixtures. It's usually easy to see the parts of a physical mixture. And you can separate the parts. To separate milk from cereal, simply pour the mixture into a strainer. The milk pours through, and the cereal stays behind. Voilà! You've separated the physical mixture!

Then put the mixture back together, and finish your breakfast!

Disappearing Matters

A second type of mixture occurs when a solid is **absorbed** into a liquid. When a solid is absorbed completely, it is dissolved. A solid cube of sugar will dissolve in hot water. But even though the solid is now invisible, its molecules are still there. When one substance is dissolved into another, the mixture is called a solution. All solutions are mixtures, but not all mixtures are solutions.

Could this be the secret to invisibility cloaks?

Are you the answer to my problem?

I'm not that kind of solution.

MIXTURE

SOLUTION

Solutions are **translucent**. Put them in a glass container, and you can see through them. A solution can be colorless like salt water. It can also be colored like Kool-Aid. Sweetened tea is a solution of tea, water, and sugar. Sodas are solutions of sugar, water, and carbon dioxide.

 Sodas are solutions of matter in all three states. Then they become a solution to thirst!

absorb—to soak up
translucent—partially see-through

It's a Party!

You mingle at parties. Molecules mingle in a solution. They distribute evenly throughout the mixture. Think of a glass of sweetened tea. It has the same number of tea, water, and sugar molecules no matter where you sip.

Molecules in mixtures get very close. But they never join to create new molecules. In a glass of tea you can't see the white sugar, clear water, or brown tea. However, the sugar, water, and tea molecules are still there. When mixed, the structures of the these molecules do not change.

Because molecules in any mixture do not change, you can always separate the ingredients. For example, a tablespoon of salt dissolved in a cup of warm water makes a solution. Can you separate the dissolved salt from the water? Sure. Put the salt water in a pan, and bring it to a boil. The liquid water turns to steam. Keep boiling! When all the water has escaped as steam, a white coating of salt is left on the bottom of the pan. Scrape up the salt, and capture the steam. You'll find you have the same amounts of salt and water that you started with.

Got matter? Of course you do. Just take a look around. From cold milk to warm cookies, matter is right at your fingertips. In fact, matter IS your fingertips!

Everything that is animal, vegetable, and mineral in all the world is made of matter. And it's all working like clockwork. Solids thump and clunk, liquids splash and flow, gases swirl and sometimes smell. This book is solid in your hands, and you're here to read it. There's nothing the matter with this matter!

Glossary

absorb (ab-ZORB)—to soak up

attract (uh-TRAKT)—to pull something toward something else

bond (BAHND)—the exchange or sharing of electrons by atoms to form a molecule

energy (EN-ur-jee)—the ability to do work, such as moving things or giving heat or light

friction (FRIK-shuhn)—a force created when two objects rub together; friction slows down objects

gaseous (GASH-uhss)—in the form of a gas

rigid (RIJ-id)—stiff and difficult to bend

translucent (trans-LOO-suhnt)—partially see-through; allowing some rays of light to pass through

volume (VOL-yuhm)—the amount of space taken up by an object

Read More

Dicker, Katie. *Properties of Matter*. Sherlock Bones Looks at Physical Science. New York: Windmill Books, 2011.

Monroe, Tilda. *What Do You Know about States of Matter?* 20 Questions. Physical Science. New York: PowerKids Press, 2011.

Slingerland, Janet. *Werewolves and States of Matter*. Monster Science. Mankato, Minn.: Capstone Press, 2012.

Internet Sites

FactHound offers a safe, fun way to find Internet sites related to this book. All of the sites on FactHound have been researched by our staff.

Here's all you do:

Visit *www.facthound.com*

Type in this code: 9781429684279

Check out projects, games and lots more at
www.capstonekids.com

Index

Why are fish so smart?
Bee-cause they live
in schools.

OK, we snuck in one
more bee joke. But I bet
you didn't see it coming!